The T[illegible]p Dog

Written by Penny McKinlay
Illustrated by Zara Slattery

Collins Educational
An Imprint of HarperCollins*Publishers*

There was once a city whose streets were narrow and black with grime, where the sun could not pierce the gloom even on the brightest day, and no-one looked up to the blue skies above.

The people of that city lived miserable lives, working so hard and so long they hardly noticed day turn to night, or night turn to day. They never had holidays or took their children out to the green fields beyond the city, so the soot on the stones and the hard cobbles beneath their bare feet were all the children knew.

Towering above this city was a palace so tall that no-one ever saw the little princess who lived inside. The princess's parents had died when she was very young, leaving her in the care of a council of advisers who did a lot of advising, but not much caring, and one faithful friend, Vita.

The princess had only once in her life been outside the palace, and she had been so terrified by people staring at her that she ordered the coach straight back home. As soon as she was safely back at the palace, she had called for her advisers and ordered them to build a great, stone wall around the palace. Every day her fear had grown, and every day she called her advisers and said, “The walls must be higher, build them higher!”

And so, day and night, the people of the city had laboured to build the wall around the palace higher.

Now one day into this sad city there came the very smallest old lady that ever lived, and walking at her heels was the very largest dog that ever lived.

The old lady's face was as rosy and wrinkled as an apple that has been left too long in the sunshine but which inside is still sweet and juicy. Her clothes were as clean and fresh as if they had just blown in off the washing-line.

The dog padded silently beside her, its great shaggy head level with the neat bun in her silvery hair. The dog had feet as big as footstools and golden fur which rippled down as thick as treacle. Its huge eyes gleamed as soft as moonstones.

Nobody watched them go by, though they were as strange a sight as a sunbeam in those dismal streets. And nobody saw them stop outside the old toy shop. For despite their hard work, no-one in this city had money to spare to buy toys and the shop had been empty as long as anyone could remember.

The tiny old lady lifted the latch and went in, followed by the dog, and the door closed silently behind them.

From the moment the shop felt her delicate touch on the rusty latch and the swish of the dog's mighty tail against the doorpost, the shop began to change. Without the use of a scrubbing brush or the lick of a paintbrush, the soot fell away and the woodwork grew bright.

When the next morning dawned fair above the rooftops, the walls were the colour of cream and the paintwork shone as red as ripe cherries.

The old lady came out to inspect the shop. She stood back, and smiled with satisfaction. Then she went in and came out with the dog, which was carrying a gleaming new shop sign in its mouth. The sign said simply:

Hearts' Desire Toys
Proprietor
Mrs Pippin

Hearts' Desire Toys
Proprietor
Mrs Dippin

Mrs Pippin, for that was the old lady's name, hopped nimbly onto the dog's back and, reaching high, hooked the sign up above the door. Then they went back inside.

A merry breeze sprang up and danced down the street to greet the new sign which creaked and swung gaily in reply. For the first time in many years people lifted their heads, their pale faces breaking into smiles at the happy sound.

As the day went on, curious children gathered round and peered in through the toy shop window. But all they could see were strange shapes and bright colours the like of which they had never before seen.

That night the children asked their work-weary parents, "Can we go to the toy shop?" But their parents sighed, "No. For toys cost money and we have none to spare."

Hearts Desire Toys
Proprietor Mrs Pippin

Even so, the next day the children gathered outside the shop again. This time the cherry-red door stood open wide. They drew close, but then jumped back with fear. For there, lying across the threshold, was the most enormous dog they had ever seen. And the only way in was over its immense back.

The dog's massive head rested on colossal paws and though it seemed to be sleeping, now and then it lazily lifted its eyelids and gazed at them with moonstone eyes. Standing just behind the dog was the tiniest old lady they had ever seen.

"Would you like to come in, children?" smiled Mrs Pippin. The children nodded their heads.
"Then why don't you?"

"We're scared of that great big dog, ma'am... and our mums and dads said we have no money to spare to buy toys."

Mrs Pippin looked at them with eyes that danced like black diamonds and said, “You don’t need money in this shop. All you need is imagination.

“And as for the dog, you’ll just have to decide which is the bigger – Molly, or your curiosity.”

Slowly and silently the children sidled closer. One by one they stepped wide over Molly and safely into the shop. All, that is, except little Joanie, who tripped and fell right onto Molly’s back! The other children gasped in fear as Molly turned her head...

… and licked Joanie with a tongue like red velvet. Joanie flung her short arms around Molly's neck and soon all the children had climbed on her broad back, too.

Molly's fur warmed them as they had never been warmed before and tickled them until they laughed as they had never laughed before, and Mrs Pippin's apple-cheeks grew rosier and more creased than ever at the sight of that heaving heap of happy children.

At last Mrs Pippin clapped her hands and something very like stardust showered from her fingertips. "Now for the serious business, children. Toys!"

The children gazed about the shop for the first time. Whichever way they looked, the shop, so tiny from the outside, went on forever. They looked up and the shelves reached endlessly on until they were lost in mist. They looked straight ahead and it seemed you could follow the shelves all your life and never find the end.

The toys that were piled upon those shelves were the toys of wildest imagination, and they appeared one by one as if by magic.

There were boxes of bricks that built castles of unsurpassed splendour, with fire-breathing dragons and armies of tiny knights fighting battles where no-one was hurt. There were dressing-up clothes in which they could become whatever they chose for just as long as they wanted. There were train sets with track that stretched for miles, and stations where passengers got on and off and ate egg sandwiches.

The children played with whatever they chose, and nobody shouted, “That’s mine!” for no-one needed to be selfish.

The children played on and on forgetting everything, while outside in the grimy streets the grey hours ground on. They played until, at last, their parents wound their weary way home from work – to empty houses. All the mothers and fathers ran into the street shouting, “Where are our children?”

The parents began to search for the children. Eventually, they came to the street with the toy shop and there they stood and gasped. Only yesterday the street had been as dark and dreary as the rest of the city. Now it was lined with cherry trees frothing with white blossom, and nested with chirruping birds. The walls of all the houses were pure cream, and the paintwork was all colours of the rainbow.

Down the street the parents strolled, gazing about them in delight, for they had not seen a single thing of beauty for many a long year. On entering the toy shop their hearts grew warm with pleasure, for there, transformed by happiness, were their children.

Some sat absorbed by their toys. Some rode on Molly as if she were a small shaggy pony, until she gently shook them, giggling, to the ground. Others gathered in raptures around Mrs Pippin who was playing a crystal xylophone. Each time she struck a note, a tiny humming bird flew up to join a brilliant flock fluttering above her head, sweetly singing.

When they saw their parents, the children ran over, and slipped their hands into theirs, speechless with the wonders of the day. They whispered their thanks to Mrs Pippin and Molly, and together the families went home in weary happiness.

That night the children fell asleep with such radiant smiles that they lit their parents' faces as they kissed them good night. There was only one child who did not smile in her sleep, and that was the little princess.

Soon the happiness the children found in the toy shop trickled out of the door and spread over the city. Streets were polished until the cobbles shone and the grime lifted away from the grey walls.

Only the palace remained untouched. The wall was now so tall that not even the birds could fly over. Soon the only living things inside were the little princess, her advisers and the one faithful friend, Vita. Only Vita was allowed in and out of the palace, to go home at night and to return in the morning. Many times the little princess stamped her foot and insisted Vita must not leave the palace, but Vita said she would be miserable if she could not go home. And so she alone, every morning and evening, passed through the great gate.

Vita was very worried about the princess. Locked up in a palace that grew daily darker as the wall blocked out more light, the princess grew ever paler until she was almost transparent. She had whole rooms full of toys she never touched. All she did was wander from window to window, ensuring that the wall was high and strong. Every day she asked, “Are you quite sure you came in alone this morning, Vita?” and Vita replied, “Yes, quite sure, little princess.”

Now, Vita had heard about the toy shop and seen the transformation in the streets.

“Well,” she thought, “if this old lady and her dog can save a whole city, surely they can help one small princess. Unless something can be done, I’m afraid the princess will become so pale, she will soon vanish.”

So that evening she went to ask Mrs Pippin and Molly for help.

“Call again tomorrow morning,” said Mrs Pippin. “We will try to help you then.”

That night the latch clicked on the toy shop door and out came Mrs Pippin and Molly. Nobody was watching as the old lady hopped onto the dog's broad back or as the dog padded silently down the street, gathering pace to a gallop until they both soared up into the sky.

Only the stars saw where Mrs Pippin and Molly went. Only the stars saw them pass snow-crested mountain tops so high they had never been scaled and skim the green valleys so secret they had never echoed to human voices. It was dawn when Mrs Pippin and Molly returned triumphantly to the toy shop carrying a toy to touch the princess's heart.

When Vita came to the shop in the morning, Mrs Pippin gave her their gift… a paintbox that painted jewel-bright pictures which came to life.

But when Vita showed the princess, the princess just said coldly, "It's only an old paintbox. Put it in the toy box with all my other toys." And she turned back again to watch for cracks in the wall.

The following night, and for many nights after, Mrs Pippin and Molly searched the heavens seeking a new toy to bring happiness to the princess. And every morning Vita would take the toy to the princess with hope it would bring her joy, only for the princess to turn away, silent.

At last one night Molly refused to go out searching any longer. She sank down on the toy shop floor and would not be moved.

But the following morning, when Vita turned sadly to go to the palace empty-handed, Molly rose and blocked her way. As Mrs Pippin and Vita watched, Molly disappeared into the boundless reaches of the shop. When at last she returned, Molly was carrying something with infinite gentleness in her soft mouth. It was a miniature Molly, a puppy with golden fur flowing like treacle and eyes glowing soft as moonstones. Vita held out her basket, and Molly set the puppy carefully inside, with a last loving lick.

“Thank you, Molly,” said Vita softly, and she gently carried the basket to the palace.

“What is it today?” asked the princess wearily, hardly bothering to turn from the window. Then came a soft yelp, and as she turned, the puppy tumbled from the basket and padded over to lick her ankles.

When the princess knelt to gather the bundle of fur in her arms, the puppy’s fur warmed her as she had never been warmed before and tickled her until she laughed as she had never laughed before. And as she laughed, the sound tinkled around the silent palace and echoed against the towering wall.

Then, a small crack appeared at the base of the wall. And another. And another. Faster and faster they raced like lightning up the wall until, with a great boom and a ragged splintering, the huge stones split open to the sun and the wall crumbled to dust.